You Are Here

You Are Here

a travel photobook

ROUGH GUIDES

Introduction

You glance across a Manhattan street and spot a modern-day Audrey Hepburn hailing a cab. You see a familiar shape emerging – the Taj Mahal, the Great Wall – through the early morning mist. You stop the hire car because your path is blocked by a pair of Shetland ponies. You stare at an Easter Island head, willing it to tell you something. You see the stillness of a heat-hazed petrol station or the Ponte 25 de Abril in Lisbon or a house on a French clifftop and it makes you feel still. You watch the chaos of a Tokyo street or Barsana's Holi festival and *that* makes you feel still. In Grindavík, Iceland, you notice a shade of green you've never seen before.

This is travel. The way that certain moments impress themselves upon us forever. Chasing these moments has always inspired Rough Guides' authors, editors and readers to get off the beaten track – and it is what inspired us to make this book. Each day, thousands upon thousands of images capturing moments like these float into digital space – but very few bypass screen fatigue to make it into print. To help us decide which ones to publish, we enlisted the curatorial judgement of experts including photography legend Martin Parr, Picfair founder Benji Lanyado, travel Instagrammer Gabriela Mateus (@gmateus), photography book specialist Bea Carvalho and Rough Guides' very own senior picture editor Phoebe Lowndes.

And by the way, Audrey's on page 44. Is she hailing a cab? Maybe, maybe not. Either way, the point is that we were captivated. So here it is: *You Are Here*, because you were there.

Rainbow Mountain, Peru
Paulius Vasaris Ruksa
@p46lo_
2016

"A local family overlooking
struggling tourists. Everyone
was having a hard time
walking, except the locals.
They were used to the altitude.
It was quite funny to see
people in their 20s on a horse
walked by locals as old as 60
or even older."

Nizwa Fort, Oman >
Phillip Grobler
@saffa_travel_teach
2016

"We found this old Omani
man sleeping at his stall. He
sells fruit and vegetables at a
market next to the fort."

11

Ko Lanta, Thailand
Laura Wozniak
@woz_photography
2017

"I'm working remotely on the lovely island of Ko Lanta for three months, and regularly miss the sunset to watch local Thais play this sport called *sepak takraw*, using a hand-woven rattan ball. Native to Southeast Asia, it's similar to footvolley in Brazil. I've become their unofficial ball girl!"

< **Oia, Santoríni, Greece**
Andrew Williams
@wilfusmcwilf
2016

Delhi, India. Robin Eley Jones. 2016.

Lofoten islands, Norway. Stephen Kotick (@satanclit). 2015.

Groningen, Netherlands. Luigi Trevisi (@luigitrevisi). 2016.

Madurai, India. Nikki Woelk (@nikki.io). 2014.

Rajasthan, India
Stephan Alberola
2017

"I took this photo while walking through a small village called Chanoud. The door is open and I see this older gentleman sitting on the floor pushing his granddaughter (or possibly great-granddaughter). They both see me and are having a great time. Now, all I have to do is to wait for the right time to capture it..."

Halifax, Nova Scotia, Canada
Ashleigh Benton
@adbentonphotography
2016

Rome, Italy
Luigi Trevisi
@luigitrevisi
2016

Taj Mahal, Agra, India. Barun Rajgaria. 2013.

Weligama, Sri Lanka. Tony Wallbank (@tonywallbank). 2017.

Rome, Italy
Jennifer Damico
@jenndamico
2011

"When in Rome, one
of my favorite things
to do is photograph
the shrines called *Le
Madonnelle* (the little
Madonnas). They are
a lovely reminder to
look up."

Rome, Italy
Manny Roman
2017

Somewhere near China
Davin Gordon
@davingordon
2017

"This little baby was touching
the window, looking out in
awe, while her mother read
a financial newspaper and
never once glanced up."

Hampi, India
Andrew Williams
@wilfusmcwilf
2016

Rajasthan, India
Annapurna Mellor
@annapurnauna
2015

"This was at the
Pushkar Camel Fair,
during a Rajasthan dance
competition where local girls
wear traditional clothes.
I spotted these four girls
backstage looking
incredibly bored."

Luang Prabang, Laos
Davide Di Salvo
2012

Tofino, British Columbia, Canada
Eric Mellor
@ericmellor
2017

"Surfers braving subzero temperatures to catch the first
waves of the new year."

Jaipur, India
Robin Eley Jones
2016

Promenade des Anglais, Nice, France. Joe Almond (@joe.almond). 2013.

New York City, USA. Natalia Radcliffe-Brine (@natalia_radcliffebrine). 2017.

Rajasthan, India
David E Smith
2017

< Rajasthan, India
Stephan Alberola
2017

Shetland, Scotland
Keith Ruffles
@keithruffles
2016

Rajasthan, India
Phoebe Baskett
@phoebebaskett
2017

"This photo was taken in Jodhpur
at the beautiful fort, a busy tourist
attraction. I caught this attendant
taking a quiet moment for himself –
perhaps for reflection, perhaps to
check his WhatsApp..."

Medersa el Attarine
Fez, Morocco
Matt Smith
@mattxfoto
2016

Consuegra, Spain
Sheralyn Graise
2016

Easter Island, Chile
Linda Bernau
@que_linda_
2015

"A once-in-a-lifetime trip to Easter Island brought me to
Rano Raraku which was used as a quarry to supply the
stone from which the Moai were carved. The slopes of this
volcanic crater are lined with many of these sculptures."

Bangkok, Thailand. Titus Scholl (@titusscholl). 2017.

Varanasi, India. Annapurna Mellor (@annapurnauna). 2016.

Tokyo, Japan. Annapurna Mellor (@annapurnauna). 2016.

Halong Bay, Vietnam. Manny Roman. 2016.

Delhi, India. Rohit Kumar.

New York City, USA. Mark Harrison. 2008.

Marrakesh, Morocco. Carlo Chinca. 2016.

Uløya, Lyngen fjord, Norway. Mark Daffey (@markdaffey). 2015.

Goa, India
Annapurna Mellor
@annapurnauna
2015

"I took the train from
South Goa to Gokarna
in India and midway
it broke down. Classic
India! I wandered
around the tracks for
a while as we waited,
and snapped this shot
through the window."

Luang Prabang, Laos
Jessica Panicola
2017

Barcelona, Spain
Solly Levi
@sollylevi
2016

Malecón, Havana, Cuba. Timothy Jones. 2011.

Lake Geneva, Switzerland. George Kerridge. 2014.

Glaciar Perito Moreno, Patagonia, Argentina. Nick Board. 2016.

Erg Chebbi dunes, Merzouga, Morocco. Claire Morris. 2012.

< Previous page:

Tarquinia, Italy
Joe Almond
@joe.almond
2013

Varadero, Cuba
Liam Klimek
@liamklimek
2016

The Louvre, Paris, France
Jo Reid
@accidental_journo
2016

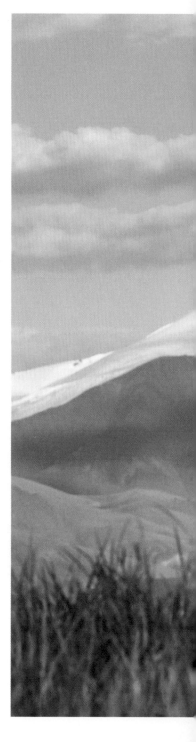

Outer Mongolia. All images by Sharon Kynaston (@sharon_kynaston_photography). 2015.

Mumbai, India
Jasmine Cook
@jascook0202
2015

Kirstenbosch National Botanical Gardens >
Cape Town, South Africa
Justin Orde
2016

< South Stack Lighthouse,
Anglesey, Wales
Tom Hirst
2015

Aksum, Ethiopia
Alex Sinclair Lack
@a_sinclairlack
2016

Venice, Italy. Ata Mohammad Adnan (@ata_md_adnan). 2014.

Thikse monastery, Ladakh, India. Udayan Sankar Pal (@UdayanSankarPal). 2013.

Syria. Claire Morris. 2009. "The Bagdad café on the road between Damascus and Homs, two years before the civil war began."

Shan State, Myanmar. Annapurna Mellor (@annapurnauna). 2014.

< Previous page:

Bwindi, Uganda
Harry Skeggs
@harryskeggs
2016

"A mountain gorilla weighs me
up from the shadowed depths
of the Bwindi jungle."

Kuala Lumpur, Malaysia >
Natalie Wright
@natalme
2017

Chennai, India. Roshan Santhosh (@swaminathan2393). 2016.

Tartu, Estonia. Piers McEwan (@onethinkingman). 2017.

Cambrian Mountains, Wales. Daniela Pardo Reyes (@imdanielapardo). 2015.

Dubai, UAE. Csilla Tornallyay (@csillatornallyay). 2017.

Fez, Morocco
Joe Almond
@joe.almond
2016

"A leather tanner crosses
colourful vats of dye
in the medina of Fez.
Following the traditional
process, hides are
soaked for two to three
days before the tanner
kneads them with his feet,
eventually leaving them
to dry in the sun."

Athens, Greece
John Puffer
1997

Grindavík, Iceland >
Meghan M. Brennan
@megzinator
2015

Guangzhou, China
Ata Mohammad Adnan
@ata_md_adnan
2011

Seoul, South Korea
Philip White
@phil22091991
2017

Huntington Beach Pier, California, USA. 2015.

Margaret River, Western Australia. 2014.

Burleigh Heads, Queensland, Australia. All images by Kevin Gallagher (@surfphotoguy). 2014.

< Previous page:

Havana, Cuba
Adam McDonald
@adammacphoto
2016

Varanasi, India
Angeli Go
2013

Sri Lanka
Marc Ehrenbold
2014

< Previous page:

Western Mongolia
Sharon Kynaston
@sharon_kynaston_photography
2015

"Outer Mongolia, where the vast open spaces of the steppes force you into that sense of literally being in the middle of nowhere. Where communication can take days, where nomads and livestock wander free, where eagle hunters keep their age-old traditions and summer Naadam festivals create community spirit."

Essaouira, Morocco >
Joseph C. Conlon
@josephconlon1
2011

Mũi Né, Vietnam
Matt Pasche
@pascheimages
2017

Ujjain, Madhya Pradesh, India
Annada Mallick
2016

"A group of boys from a religious school in Banaras came to the holy Shipra river for Ujjain Kumbh Mela. Here they are chanting at the time of evening bath with the help of their teacher."

Nandgaon, Uttar Pradesh, India. Yakov Pavlov (@ygpavlov). 2017.

Bawame, Oro Province, Papua New Guinea. Stephen Walford. 2013.

Hokkaido, Japan. Nikki Biggs. 2014.

Shanghai, China. Charlie Gross (@ctgrossp).

< Previous page:

Cavernas de Mármol, Chile
Carmen Cheung
@carmen.chameleon
2016

"The Cavernas de Mármol are located on a peninsula of
solid marble bordering Lake General Carrera, a remote
glacial lake that spans the Chile-Argentina border. It took
an internal flight, countless local buses, and a kayak to
get there but with scenery this beautiful, it was worth it.
This shot was taken from a single-person kayak."

The Alhambra, Granada, Spain >
Daina Hodgson
@dainahodgson
2016

"Capturing this couple having such a beautiful moment
was all about patience. As tourists, lovers, and adventurers
clamoured all around me I had to wait for the perfect
opportunity – and then the sea of people parted..."

Svalbard, Norway
Harry Skeggs
@harryskeggs
2015

"A polar bear treads a
lonely path, king in a
barren world of white."

Hong Kong, China
Richard Forbes-Hamilton
@highestlearning
2016

Turin, Italy
Georgina Chrisp
@gchrispy
2016

Inle Lake, Myanmar (Burma)
Robin Eley Jones
2015

Dubrovnik, Croatia
Finola Farrell
@finfarrell
2016

Cartagena, Colombia
Nicol Nicolson
@nicolnic
2016

Lulworth Cove, Dorset, England. 2014.

Perhentian Islands, Malaysia. 2015.

Bako National Park, Borneo. 2015.

Perhentian Islands, Malaysia. All images by Freya Cardiff (@freyavc). 2015.

Williamsburg Bridge, New York, USA. Chris Dixie. 2016.

Lisbon, Portugal. Emanuel Pereira Aparicio Ribeiro (@emanuelparibeiro). 2014.

Dalian, China. Mark Harrison. 2006.

Toronto, Canada. James Hackland (@james.hackland). 2014.

< Previous page:

Rome, Italy
Bob Berry
2013

"On a visit to the Vatican and a climb to the top of
St Peter's, I noticed people crossing this courtyard
and the strong symbolic shadows being cast. After a
twenty minute wait, the nun walked into the shot."

Reine, Norway
Lindsay Steele
@lasphotos
2017

Kerala, India
Laura Giri
@lauragiriphotography
2016

< Previous page:

Spiti Valley, India
Nimit Nigam
@nimitnigam
2016

Yunnan, China >
Pauline Guerreau
2017

Santa Teresa, Costa Rica. Nick Jamison (@njamison). 2016.

Mombasa, Kenya. Gwen Blatz. 2017.

Angkor, Cambodia. Manuel Guerra. 2016.

Oaxaca, Mexico. Angeli Go. 2008.

Lisbon, Portugal
Sara Stromberg
@sara.stromberg
2015

Midway, Utah, USA
Amanda Kogan
@developed.moments
2017

Reyniskirkja, Reynisfjara, Iceland

Reykjavík, Iceland

Kerið, Iceland

Skógafoss waterfall, Iceland. All images by Tatianna Ducklow (@tatiannaducklow). 2017.

Venice, Italy. John Puffer. 1995.

West Bengal, India. Somenath Mukhopadhyay. 2017.

New York City, USA. Jumar Mundo (@moon.doe). 2015.

West Bengal, India. Somenath Mukhopadhyay. 2015.

Leh, India
Udayan Sankar Pal
@UdayanSankarPal
2013

"A gentle S-shaped river appearing out of the depths of the Himalayan mountains. Nature manifests itself in all its gorgeous hues, the Indus in an ethereal blue, the Zanskar River in aqua green, the golden sands, mossy brown and rust coloured landscape. Nature's painting at its best!"

Cádiz, Spain. Aya Okawa (@labyrinthiansmile). 2016.

Los Angeles, California, USA. Stuart Wilson. 2016.

Batticaloa, Sri Lanka. Joseph C. Conlon (@josephconlon1). 2016.

Omo Valley, Ethiopia. Robin Yong (@travel_portraits). 2016.

Parque Nacional Torres del Paine, Chile
Vair Jennifer Pointon
@vairbear
2011

Antelope Canyon, Arizona, USA
Mrinal Mohit
@wowitsmrinal
2016

< Previous page:

Habra, West Bengal, India
Sandipani Chattopadhyay
@sandipanichattopadhyay
2016

Canning, West Bengal, India
Sandipani Chattopadhyay
@sandipanichattopadhyay
2015

Dakshin Barasat, West Bengal, India
Pranab Basak
2016

Bagan, Myanmar (Burma). All images by Gavin Burnett (@9avin). 2012.

Trinidad, Cuba. Andrew Williams (@wilfusmcwilf). 2016.

Portland Street, Hong Kong, China. Gerrit Swanepoel (@ruthven222). 2016.

Banda Temple, West Bengal, India. Ujjal Kumar Das. 2017.

Zhangjiajie National Forest Park, Hunan Province, China. Stephanie du Plessis (@antsypantsphotography). 2017.

Dubrovnik, Croatia
Ida Huntic
@idahuntic
2016

London, England
Josh Hammond
@joshhammond4
2017

< Previous page:

Muslim Quarter, Xi'an, China
Shaun Yardley
@shaunyardley
2017

Viñales, Cuba >
Matthew Cherchio
@matthew.cherchio
2017

"A man sorts dried tobacco leaves in Viñales, Cuba.
Viñales claims to be home of the finest tobacco in Cuba
(and by extension the world) due to the iron-rich soil and
other favorable growing conditions found there."

Sahara Desert, Mergouza, Morocco
Daina Hodgson
@dainahodgson
2016

"When I drove into the small town of Merzouga near the Algerian border, my heart skipped. I felt I had been dropped on another planet. The pink, camel, and rich browns of the huge dune expanse north of town danced before us and we organized a local guide for the next day. In our bare feet we wandered through the sands, the sun beating down and the dryness constricting our throats. Out of nowhere, a young boy walked before us and then away again into the swirl of sand like a nomadic dream."

< Gaping Gill, Yorkshire Dales, England
Nick Ledger
2015

< Previous page:

Yick Fat Building, Hong Kong, China
Javier Blanco
@awoisoak
2016

Rio de Janeiro, Brazil
Ben Goodwin
2014

Siem Reap, Cambodia
Carol Moir
@caroljmoir
2017

**Barsana,
Uttar Pradesh, India**
Debdatta Chakraborty
2016

"Barsana is believed
to be the home of
the mythological
character of Lord
Krishna, around
whom the entire
saga of Holi is woven
in India – Holi is
celebrated at its
wildest at Barsana."

Myanmar (Burma)
Melissa Johnson-Peters
@silvercatphotography
2013

"I met this friendly Pa-O
villager on the Inle
Lake-Kalaw trek. Like
many young locals she
was initially on the hunt
for sweets from tourists,
but after I showed her
a few shots, she loved
posing for the camera
and was fascinated by
the images of herself."

Southern Queensland,
Australia
Matt Murray
@mattloves
2017

147

Petra, Jordan
Steven Martin
@stevesayskanpai
2017

**U Bein Bridge,
Myanmar**
Natalie Sanderson
2017

**Lago Argentino, El
Calafate, Argentina**
Matthew Cherchio
@matthew.cherchio
2017

Fez, Morocco
Joe Almond
@joe.almond

"Wandering through the narrow streets of the ninth-century medina in Fez, the unexpected sight of a young boy on horseback came in to view. I was able to capture the moment before his father loaded the final goods and they weaved onwards towards the morning market."

Giza, Egypt. Ed Lancaster. 2017.

St Petersburg, Russia. Al Lapkovsky. 2013.

**Ponte 25 de Abril,
Lisbon, Portugal**
Ruth Vatcher
@ruthvatcher
2016

155

< Previous page:

Langdale Valley,
Lake District, England
Andrew Clayborough
2012

Puglia, Italy
Finola Farrell
@finfarrell
2017

Preikestolen, Norway
Agathe Monnot
@agathelecaillou
2014

Bali, Indonesia
Apratim Sahu
@apratimclicks
2017

< **Sequoia National Park, California, USA**
Audrey Jestin
2008

Garibaldi Provincial Park, British Columbia, Canada. Louis Gabriel Kéroack (@lgkeroack). 2017.

Angkor Wat, Cambodia. Stuart Forster. 2014.

Bangkok, Thailand. Manuel Guerra. 2016.

Crozon, France. Agathe Monnot (@agathelecaillou). 2016.

< Previous page:

Lake Ashi, Hakone, Japan
Aga Kozmic
@aga_amatteroftaste
2016

Trinidad, Cuba
Nazleen Karim
@littlehumandetail
2017

Jambiani, Zanzibar, Tanzania
Chris Dixie
2015

Varanasi, India
Nimit Nigam
@nimitnigam
2016

Fushimi-Inari Taisha, Kyoto, Japan >
Geoff Moen
@gmoen7
2017

**Shilabati River,
West Bengal, India**
Deba Prasad Roy
@dpr_image
2014

171

Marrakesh, Morocco
Natalia Radcliffe-Brine
@natalia_radcliffebrine
2017

< **West Bengal, India**
Nimai Chandra Ghosh
2010

Kolkata, West Bengal, India. Rhys Williams (@swilatse5). 2017.

Dom Pedro IV square, Lisbon, Portugal. Richard Forbes-Hamilton (@highestlearning). 2014.

Cartagena, Colombia. Al Lapkovsky. 2009.

Paris, France. Mujahid Kidwai (@mujahidkidwai). 2015.

Reykjavík, Iceland
Jon Hayes
@jono7607
2017

< **Hill of Crosses, Lithuania**
Virginia Chico
@ginnychico
2012

< Previous page:

Thessalía, Greece
Ollie Taylor
@ollietaylorphotography
2017

Varanasi, India >
Nimai Chandra Ghosh
2002

Loch Coruisk, Isle of Skye, Scotland. Steven Oakes (@stevenoakes79). 2016.

Havana, Cuba. James Hackland (@james.hackland). 2016.

Wailing Wall, Jerusalem. Garry Blatz. 2015.

Shanghai, China. Nick Jamison (@njamison). 2014.

< Previous page:

Kawah Putih, Indonesia
Angeli Go
2013

Havana, Cuba >
Adam McDonald
@adammacphoto
2016

"After two weeks roaming across the island,
I arrived in Havana just in time for Obama's
historic visit and the free Rolling Stones concert.
My Cuba shots will always remind me of a very
accidental, once-in-a-lifetime experience."

Gdańsk Shipyard, Poland. Stefka Lukyj. 2017.

Solna Centrum metro, Stockholm, Sweden. Reuben Griffiths (@reuben_gee). 2013.

Alappuzha, Kerala, India. Norman Burns. 2016.

Hoi An, Vietnam. Kelvin Nuñez (@alch.emy).

**Durbete in Amhara, near Bahir
Dar, Ethiopia**
Raïsa Mirza
@raimirza
2017

Neist Point, Isle of Skye, Scotland
Emma Hall
@efrancisadventure
2017

< Previous page:

Kerala, India
Margaret Soraya
@margaretsoraya
2016

Lalibela, Ethiopia
Alex Sinclair Lack
@a_sinclairlack
2016

Preah Nimith waterfall, Preah Vihear, Cambodia
Jess Newell
@_jessnewell
2016

Paris, France
Alex Baillie
@bailliephotogr
2014

Amboseli, Kenya
Jordi Morera
@jordi_morera
2017

Sydney, Australia. Dominic Burdon. 2016.

Salento, Colombia. Hilary Kennedy (@hiltown_). 2017.

Atlin, Northern British Columbia, Canada. Harriet Hadfield (@harriet.hadfield). 2017.

Pyongyang, North Korea. Eric Mellor (@ericmellor). 2017.

< Previous page:

Dubai, UAE
Mujahid Kidwai
@mujahidkidwai
2017

Cartagena, Colombia
Al Lapkovsky
2009

U Bein Bridge, Myanmar
Natalie Sanderson
2017

Ho Chi Minh City, Vietnam. Matthew Pasche (@pascheimages). 2017.

Venice, Italy. Eric Baldauf. 2012.

Positano, Italy. Mark Harrison. 2011.

Varanasi, India. Jenny Downing. 2015.

Copenhagen, Denmark
Chris Dixie
2015

Ilıcak near Beytüşşebap, Turkey
Joe Steele
2016

< Previous page:

**Sri Meenakshi Temple,
Madurai, India**
Marty Mellway
@martymellway
2011

St. Florian's Gate, Kraków, Poland
India-Jayne Trainor
@indiajayne_photography
2016

Brooklyn Heights, New York City
Manuel Guerra
2015

Khadakwasla Dam, near Pune, India. Balram Tiwari (@balram_tiwari). 2017.

Marrakesh, Morocco. Sara Stromberg (@sara.stromberg). 2015.

Manchester, England. Beth Owen (@beth.owen_mcr). 2015.

Bali, Indonesia. Kellie Netherwood (@kellienetherwood). 2016.

Beiling Park, Shenyang, China
Holly Mather
@holls_wandering
2015

Old Havana, Cuba
Milla Muginova
2017

Rough Guide credits

Editor: Neil McQuillian
Design and layout: Nathan Watson
Picture editor: Phoebe Lowndes
Proofreaders: Helen Abramson, Greg Dickinson, Ros Walford and Aimee White
Managing editor: Monica Woods

Production: Alex Bell, Jimmy Lao and Igrain Roberts
Editorial assistant: Aimee White
Senior DTP coordinator: Dan May
Programme manager: Gareth Lowe
Publishing director: Georgina Dee

Publishing information

Distributed by Penguin Random House

Penguin Books Ltd, 80 Strand, London WC2R 0RL
Penguin Group (USA), 345 Hudson Street, NY 10014, USA
Penguin Group (Australia), 250 Camberwell Road, Camberwell, Victoria 3124, Australia
Penguin Group (NZ), 67 Apollo Drive, Mairangi Bay, Auckland 1310, New Zealand
Penguin Group (South Africa), Block D, Rosebank Office Park, 181 Jan Smuts Avenue, Parktown North, Gauteng, South Africa 2193
Rough Guides is represented in Canada by DK Canada, 320 Front Street West, Suite 1400, Toronto, Ontario M5V 3B6

© 2017 Rough Guides

1 3 5 7 9 8 6 4 2

216pp includes index

A catalogue record for this book is available from the British Library
ISBN: 978-0-24131-791-4

Contributors

Thanks to everyone who entered the 2017 Rough Guides travel photography competition for a chance to be featured in *You Are Here*.

Jacket image: Solly Levi

pp.2–3: Danielle Lancaster

p.4: Marc Ehrenbold

Special mentions from the judging panel:

Joe Almond; Pranab Basak; Ashleigh Benton; Bob Berry; Javier Blanco; Dominic Burdon; Gavin Burnett; Freya Cardiff; Debdatta Chakraborty; Jenny Downing; Nimai Chandra Ghosh; Manuel Guerra; James Hackland; Nazleen Karim; Sharon Kynaston; Al Lapkovsky; Adam McDonald; Piers McEwan; Annapurna Mellor; Geoff Moen; Milla Muginova; Somenath Mukhopadhyay; Yakov Pavlov; Deba Prasad Roy; Paulius Vasaris Ruksa; Sara Stromberg; Balram Tiwari; George Turner; Shaun Yardley.

All others whose work is featured:

Ata Mohammad Adnan; Stephan Alberola; Nick Anderson; Alex Baillie; Eric Baldauf; Phoebe Baskett; Linda Bernau; Nikki Biggs; Garry Blatz; Gwen Blatz; Nick Board; Meghan M. Brennan; Norman Burns; Sandipani Chattopadhyay; Matthew Cherchio; Carmen Cheung; Virginia Chico; Carlo Chinca; Georgina Chrisp; Andrew Clayborough; Joseph C. Conlon; Jasmine Cook; Mark Daffey; Jennifer Damico; Ujjal Kumar Das; Davide Di Salvo; Chris Dixie; Tatianna Ducklow; Finola Farrell; Richard Forbes-Hamilton; Stuart Forster; Kevin Gallagher; Laura Giri; Angeli Go; Ben Goodwin; Davin Gordon; Sheralyn Graise; Reuben Griffiths; Phillip Grobler; Charlie Gross; Pauline Guerreau; Harriet Hadfield; Emma Hall; Mark Harrison; Jon Hayes; Tom Hirst; Daina Hodgson; Josh Hammond; Ida Huntic; Nick Jamison; Audrey Jestin; Melissa Johnson-Peters; Robin Eley Jones; Timothy Jones; Hilary Kennedy; Louis Gabriel Kéroack; George Kerridge; Mujahid Kidwai; Liam Klimek; Amanda Kogan; Stephen Kotick; Aga Kozmic; Rohit Kumar; Alex Sinclair Lack; Ed Lancaster; Nick Ledger; Stefka Lukyj; Annada Mallick; Steven Martin; Holly Mather; Eric Mellor; Marty Mellway; Raïsa Mirza; Mrinal Mohit; Carol Moir; Agathe Monnot; Jordi Morera; Claire Morris; Jumar Mundo; Matt Murray; Kellie Netherwood; Jess Newell; Nicol Nicolson; Nimit Nigam; Kelvin Nuñez; Steven Oakes; Aya Okawa; Justin Orde; Beth Owen; Udayan Sankar Pal; Joe Steele; Jessica Panicola; Matt Pasche; Stephanie du Plessis; Vair Jennifer Pointon; John Puffer; Natalia Radcliffe-Brine; Barun Rajgaria; Jo Reid; Daniela Pardo Reyes; Matthew Pasche; Emanuel Pereira Aparicio Ribeiro; Manny Roman; Keith Ruffles; Apratim Sahu; Natalie Sanderson; Roshan Santhosh; Titus Scholl; Harry Skeggs; David E Smith; Matt Smith; Margaret Soraya; Lindsay Steele; Gerrit Swanepoel; Ollie Taylor; Csilla Tornallyay; India-Jayne Trainor; Luigi Trevisi; Ruth Vatcher; Stephen Walford; Tony Wallbank; Philip White; Andrew Williams; Rhys Williams; Stuart Wilson; Nikki Woelk; Laura Wozniak; Natalie Wright; Robin Yong.